EARLY TO MID-INTERMEDIATE

ACCENT ON CLASSICAL

BY WILLIAM GILLOCK

**NINE
TIMELESS
CLASSICS**

ISBN 978-1-4584-1933-0

WILLIS MUSIC

EXCLUSIVELY DISTRIBUTED BY

HAL•LEONARD®
CORPORATION
7777 W. BLUEMOUND RD. P.O. BOX 13819 MILWAUKEE, WI 53213

Visit Hal Leonard Online at
www.halleonard.com

FOREWORD

This compilation of William Gillock pieces was inspired by the composer's clear love for the classics. It is undeniable that Gillock's music, much of it composed in the mid to late 20th century, is deserving of an entirely new generation of performers and enthusiasts. These new engravings aim to preserve Gillock's original intent and musical purpose.

While a few pieces in this collection may be less familiar, certainly all are worthy of study. Beethoven's "Für Elise" and "German Dance" are made accessible for the early intermediate student, as is Tchaikovsky's famous "March" from the *Nutcracker*. All are appealingly arranged. "Etude," his energetic nod to Carl Czerny, is thoroughly infectious and a joy to play. The mini masterpiece "Homage to Chopin" was first published in the 1964 collection *Accent on the Black Keys* as an exercise towards mastering the challenging key of G-sharp minor. The title was spelled the French way, i.e. "hommage." Almost 30 years later Gillock would revise the piece for inclusion in *Collected Short Lyric Pieces*; it is the revised version in G minor that is featured here. The final piece in the collection, Gillock's "Sonatina in C," was also revisited in a second printing several years after its first publication – it originally appeared in *Accent on Analytical Sonatinas* as the first sonatina (of three). The other pieces in this collection – "Barcarolle," "Piece in Classic Style," and "Capriccietto" – are equally enchanting and performance-worthy.

CONTENTS

Für Elise

Ludwig van Beethoven
(1770–1827)
Arranged by William Gillock

Andante comodo

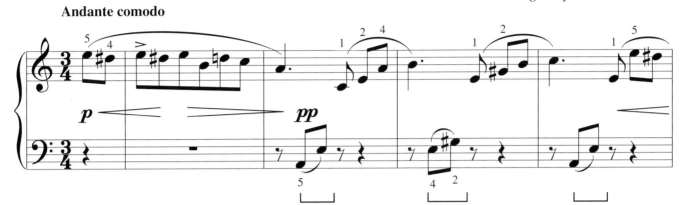

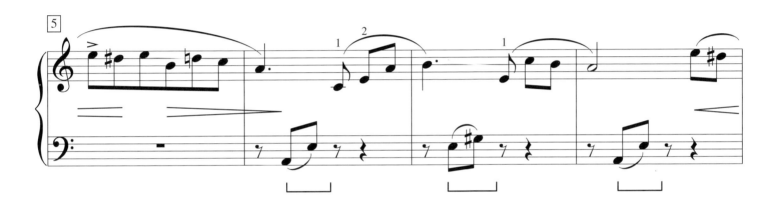

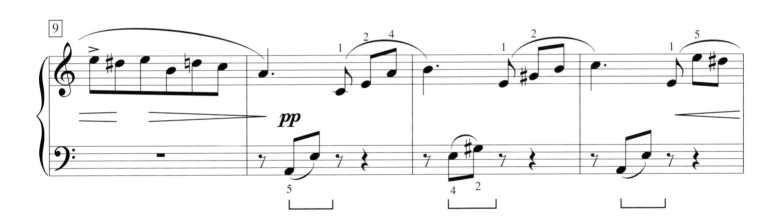

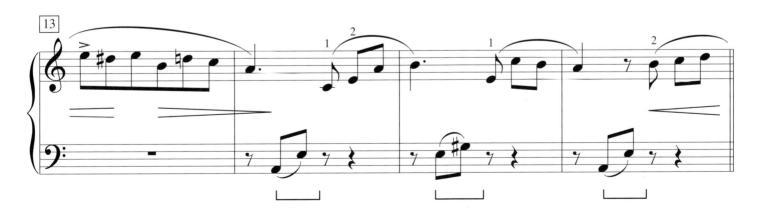

For the Junior Pianists' Guild of Dallas, Texas

German Dance
Op. 17, No.9

Ludwig van Beethoven
(1770–1827)
Transcribed and arranged by
William Gillock

Lively waltz tempo

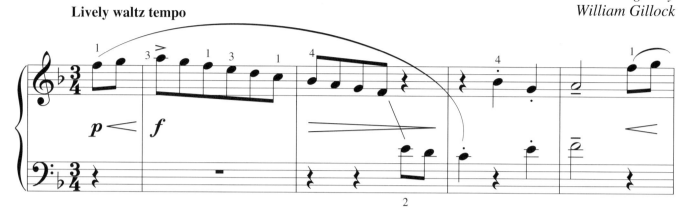

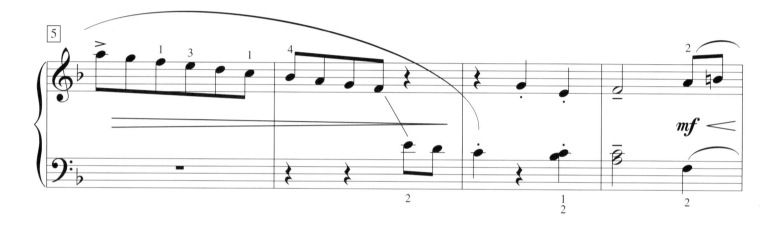

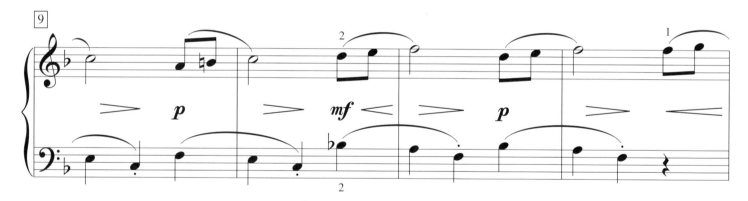

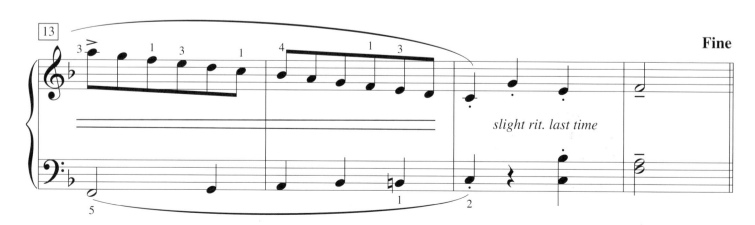

17 **TRIO**

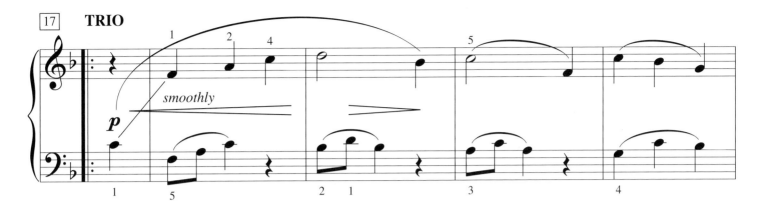

smoothly
p

21

25

f robustly accented

29

D.C. al Fine

Piece in Classic Style

William Gillock

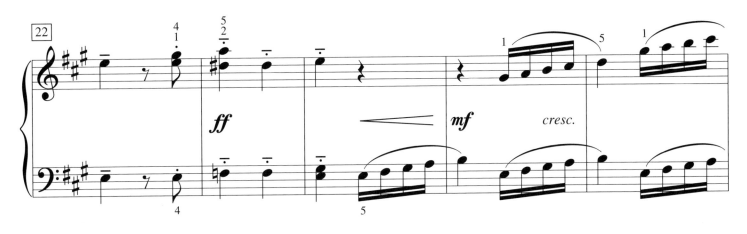

Capriccietto

William Gillock

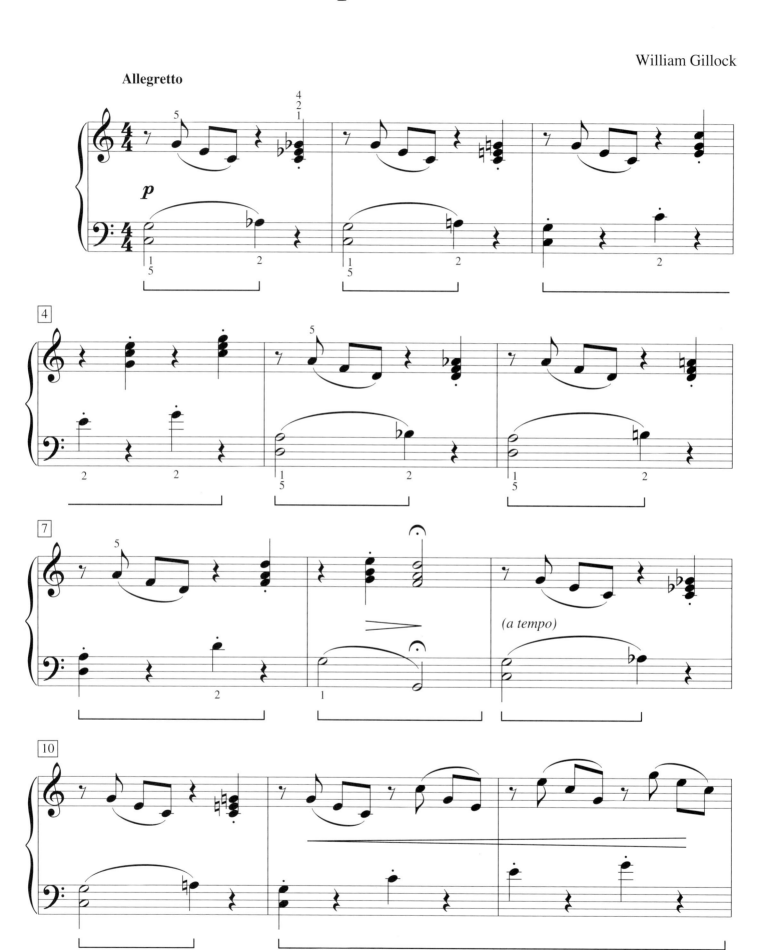

*Italian for "short"

Etude
(In the Style of Czerny)

Carl Czerny
1791–1857

William Gillock

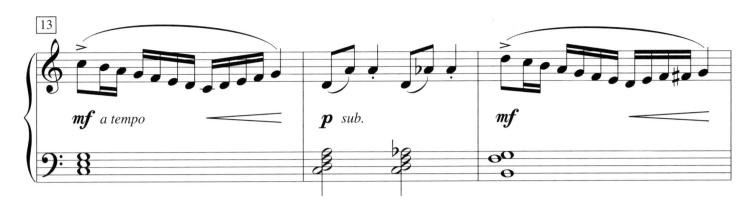

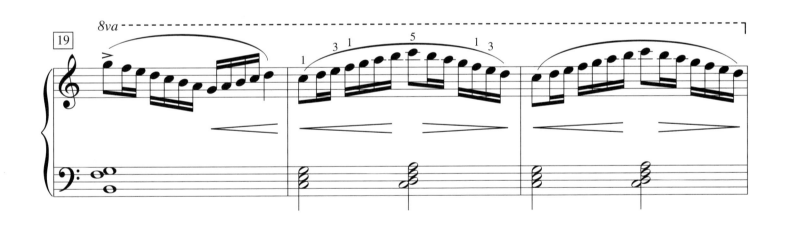

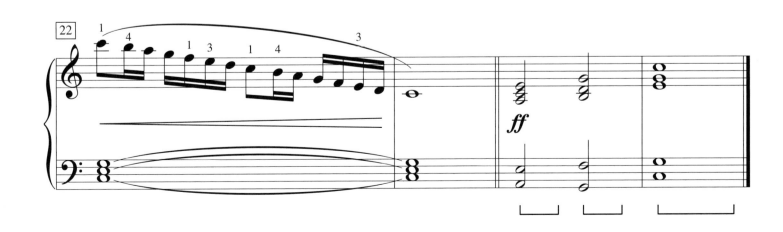

For Catherine Rollin

Homage to Chopin*

Frédéric Chopin
1810–1849

William Gillock

Allegretto cantabile

* This piece was first published as "Hommage to Chopin" in the key of G-sharp minor.

Barcarolle

William Gillock

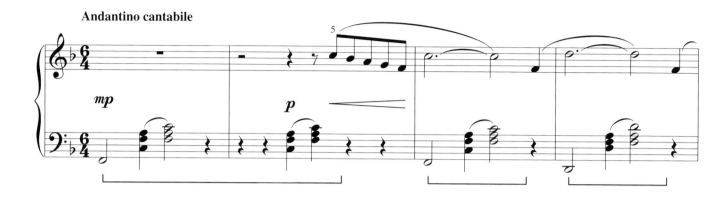

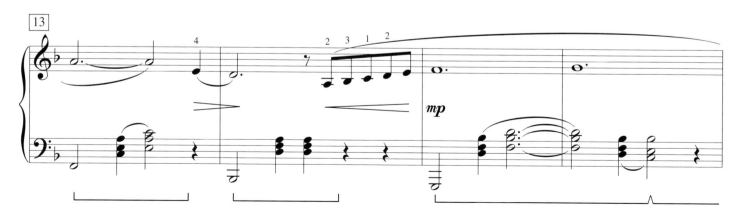

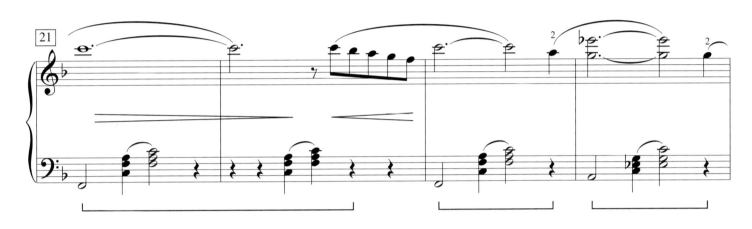

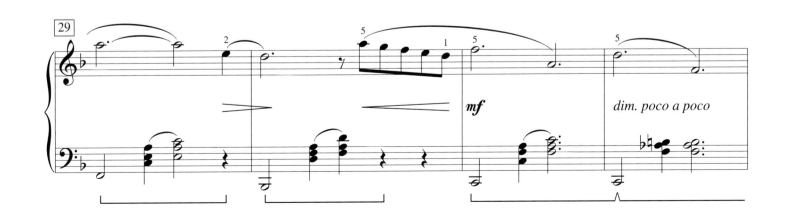

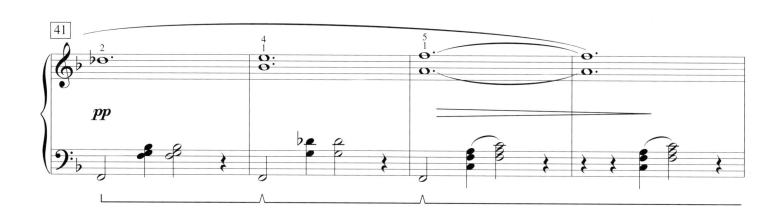

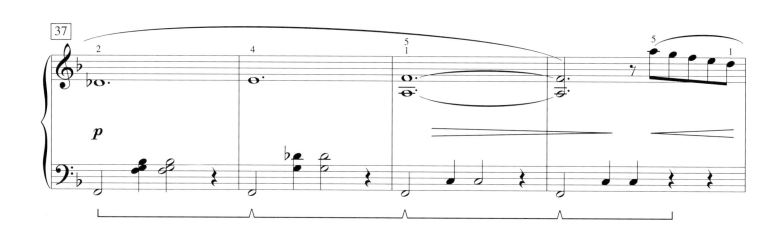

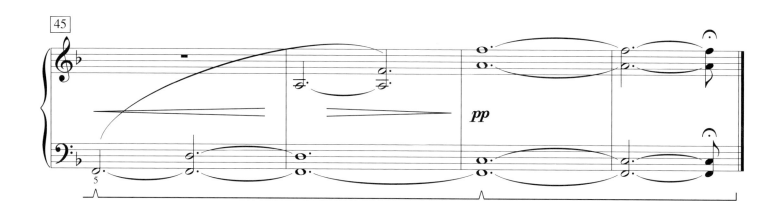

March
from THE NUTCRACKER SUITE

Pyotr I. Tchaikovsky
(1840–1893)
Transcribed by William Gillock

March tempo

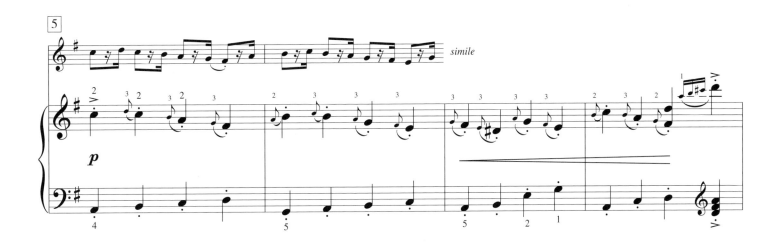

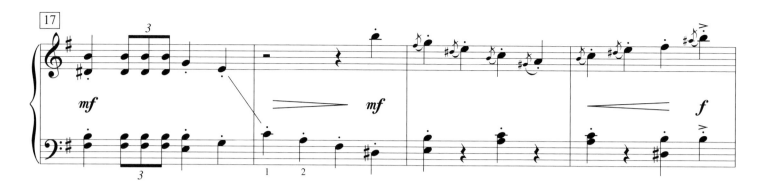

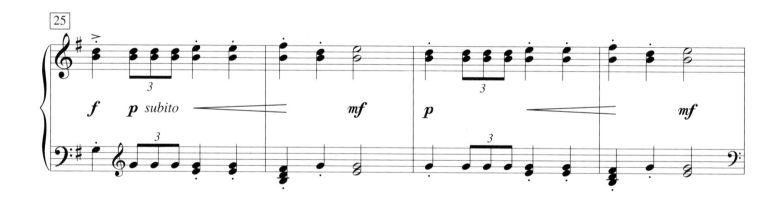

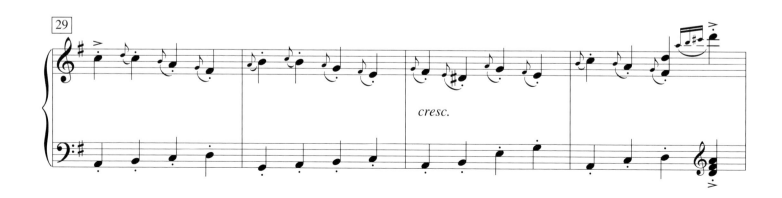

Sonatina in C

William Gillock

I. Moderato grazioso

II. Andante

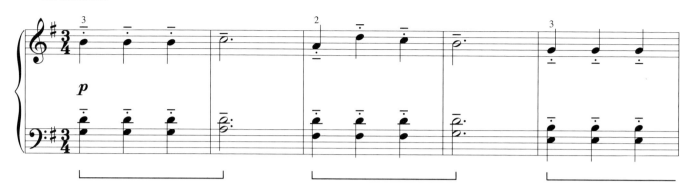

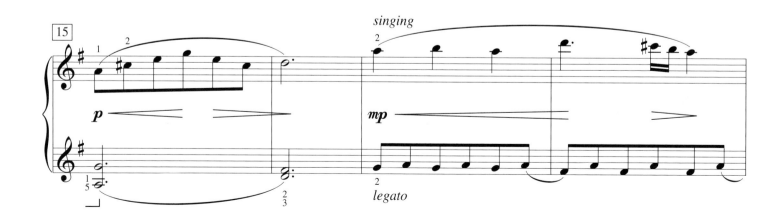

III. Vivace

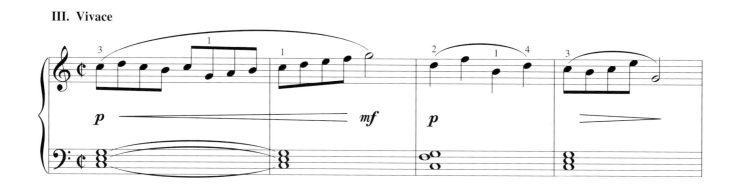

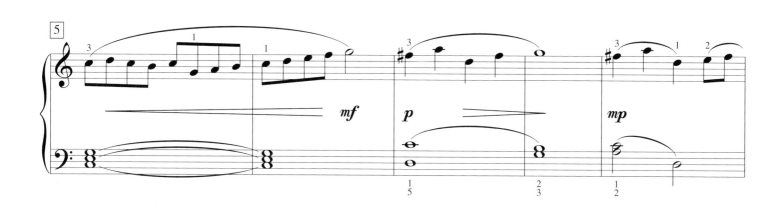

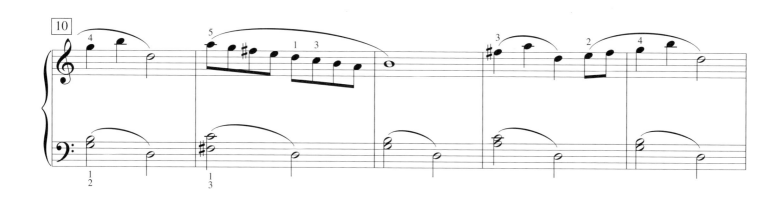

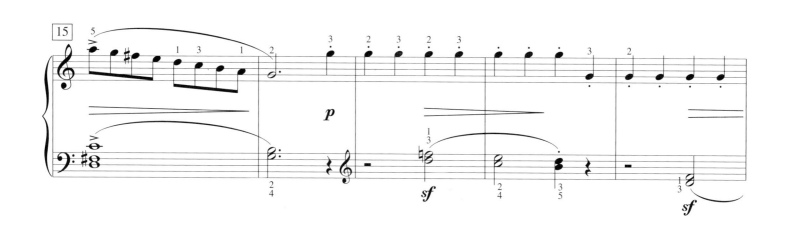

BIOGRAPHY

WILLIAM GILLOCK (1917–1993), noted music educator and composer, was born in LaRussell, Missouri, where he learned to play the piano at an early age. After graduating from Central Methodist College (now Central Methodist University), his musical career led him to long tenures in New Orleans and Dallas, where he was in high demand as a teacher, clinician, and composer. He was known as the "Schubert of children's composers" in tribute to his extraordinary melodic gift, and published numerous piano solos and ensembles for students of all levels. Renowned pedagogue and composer Lynn Freeman Olson once wrote: "The Gillock name spells magic to teachers around the world... In each Gillock composition, no matter what the teaching purpose, musical quality comes first."

Mr. Gillock was honored on multiple occasions by the National Federation of Music Clubs (NFMC) with the Award of Merit for Service to American Music, and his music remains remarkably popular throughout the United States and throughout the world.

Dynamic Duets
and Exciting Ensembles from Willis Music!

SELECTED COLLECTIONS

00416804 Accent on Duets (MI-LI) /
  William Gillock.......................$12.99

00416822 All-American Ragtime Duets
  (EI) / *Glenda Austin* $7.99

00416732 Concerto No. 1
  for Piano and Strings (MI) (2P, 4H) /
  Alexander Peskanov $14.95

00416898 Duets in Color Book 1 (EI-MI) /
  Naoko Ikeda $12.99

00138687 5 Easy Duets (EE-ME) /
  Carolyn Miller $7.99

00406230 First Piano Duets (EE) /
  John Thompson series $4.95

00416805 New Orleans Jazz Styles Duets
  (EI) / *Gillock, arr. Austin*............$9.99

00416830 Teaching Little Fingers Easy Duets
  (EE) / *arr. Miller* $6.99

SELECTED SHEETS

Early Elementary
00125695 The Knights' Quest (1P, 4H) /
  Wendy Stevens............................$3.99
00406743 Wisteria (1P, 4H) /
  Carolyn C. Setliff........................$2.95

Mid-Elementary
00412289 Andante Theme from
  "Surprise Symphony" (1P, 8H) /
  Haydn, arr. Bilbro $2.95
00406208 First Jazz (1P, 4H) /
  Melody Bober.............................$2.50

Later Elementary
00415178 Changing Places (1P, 4H) /
  Edna Mae Burnam $3.99
00406209 Puppy Pranks (1P, 4H) /
  Melody Bober.............................$2.50
00416864 Rockin' Ragtime Boogie (1P, 4H) /
  Glenda Austin.............................$3.99
00120780 Strollin' (1P, 4H) /
  Carolyn Miller.............................$3.99

Early Intermediate
00113157 Dance in the City (1P, 4H) /
  Naoko Ikeda $3.99
00416843 Festive Celebration (1P, 4H) /
  Carolyn Miller............................$3.99
00114960 Fountain in the Rain (1P, 4H) /
  William Gillock, arr. Austin........$3.99
00416854 A Little Bit of Bach (1P, 4H) /
  Glenda Austin.............................$3.99
00158602 Reflections of You (1P, 4H) /
  Randall Hartsell..........................$3.99
00416921 Tango in D Minor (IP, 4H) /
  Carolyn Miller $3.99
00416955 Tango Nuevo (1P, 4H) /
  Eric Baumgartner $3.99

Mid-Intermediate
00411831 Ave Maria (2P, 4H) /
  Bach-Gounod, arr. Hinman........$2.95
00410726 Carmen Overture (1P, 6H) /
  Bizet, arr. Sartorio......................$3.95
00404388 Champagne Toccata (2P, 8H) /
  William Gillock $3.99
00405212 Dance of the Sugar Plum Fairy /
  Tchaikovsky, arr. Gillock $3.99
00416959 Samba Sensation (1P, 4H) /
  Glenda Austin.............................$3.99
00405657 Valse Elegante (1P, 4H) /
  Glenda Austin.............................$3.99
00149102 Weekend in Paris (1P, 4H) /
  Naoko Ikeda $3.99

Later Intermediate
00415223 Concerto Americana (2P, 4H) /
  John Thompson $5.99
00405552 España Cañi (1P, 4H) /
  Marquina, arr. Gillock $3.99
00405409 March of the Three Kings
  (1P, 4H) / *Bizet, arr. Gillock*.......$2.95

Advanced
00411832 Air (2P, 4H) / *Bach,
  arr. Hinman* $2.95
00405663 Habañera (1P, 4H) /
  Stephen Griebling $2.95
00405299 Jesu, Joy of Man's Desiring
  (1P, 4H) / *Bach, arr. Gillock*.......$3.99
00405648 Pavane (1P, 4H) /
  Fauré, arr. Carroll......................$2.95

View sample pages and
hear audio excerpts online at
www.halleonard.com.

www.willispianomusic.com

Prices, contents, and availability subject to change without notice.

0617

Modern Course Supplements

CLASSICAL

Compiled and edited by Philip Low, Sonya Schumann, and Charmaine Siagian

The Classical Piano Solos series offers carefully-leveled, original piano works from Baroque to the early 20th century, featuring the simplest classics in Grade 1 to concert-hall repertoire in Grade 5. The series aims to keep with the spirit of John Thompson's legendary **Modern Course** method by providing delightful lesson and recital material that will motivate and inspire.

FIRST GRADE
Features a mix of 22 well-known pieces, including several from Bartok's method (co-authored in 1913 with Reschofsky) and Burgmüller's "Arabesque," as well as lesser-known gems by composers like Melanie Bonis, Vincent d'Indy, and Daniel Turk. Also includes two bonus pieces - by Gurlitt and Schmitt respectively - that have been adapted so that the beginning student can immediately start playing the classical repertoire.
00119738 ....$6.99

SECOND GRADE
22 original pieces from the masters! Features a mix of well-known pieces such as Petzold's "Minuet in G Major" from the Anna Magdelena Notebook, Schumann's "Soldier's March," and Beethoven's "Ecossaise in G Major," as well as lesser-known gems like d'Indy's modern "Three-Finger Partita" and Rebikov's ominous "Limping Witch Lurking in the Woods."
00119739 ....$6.99

THIRD GRADE
20 original pieces from the masters! Features a mix of well-known pieces such as Burgmüller's "Ballade" and Rebikov's "Playing Soldiers," as well as lesser-known gems like CPE Bach's "Presto" – a fast, motivating recital piece; and the lovely, lyrical "Piece Romantique" by Cecile Chaminade.
00119740 ....$7.99

FOURTH GRADE
18 original pieces from the masters! Features a mix of well-known pieces including Grieg's "Arietta" and Chopin's "Prelude in E Minor," as well as lesser-known, yet equally effective works by Teresa Carreno ("Berceuse"), Vladimir Rebikov ("The Music Lesson"), and Theodor Kullak ("The Ghost in the Fireplace").
00119741 ....$7.99

FIFTH GRADE
19 original pieces from the masters! Grade 5 features a mix of well-known pieces such as Beethoven's "Moonlight" sonata (1st mvmt) and Rachmaninoff's famous C-sharp prelude, as well as lesser-known gems from Samuel Coleridge-Taylor ("They Will Not Lend Me a Child"), Anatoly Lyadov ("Prelude in B Minor"), and Rameau ("Les niais de Sologne"). All four main periods are represented.
00119742 ....$8.99

POPULAR

Arranged by Glenda Austin, Eric Baumgartner, and Carolyn Miller

These supplementary songbooks are loaded with great songs – pop hits, Broadway and movie themes, and more! Each book correlates with a grade in **Modern Course for the Piano**, and can be used as supplementary material with any piano method.

FIRST GRADE
12 songs: Edelweiss • Fly Me to the Moon • Go the Distance • It's a Small World • Let's Go Fly a Kite • Love Me Tender • Oh, What a Beautiful Mornin' • The Rainbow Connection • This Is It • What the World Needs Now Is Love • You Are My Sunshine • You'll Be in My Heart.
00416707 Book/Audio...$12.99
00416691 Book Only..$7.99

SECOND GRADE
11 songs: The Addams Family Theme • Alley Cat • Do-Re-Mi • I Could Have Danced All Night • The Masterpiece • Memory • My Heart Will Go On • Raiders March • Nadia's Theme • Sway • A Time for Us.
00416708 Book/Audio...$12.99
00416692 Book Only..$7.99

THIRD GRADE
10 songs: Beauty and the Beast • Bibbidi-Bobbidi-Boo • Castle on a Cloud • Climb Ev'ry Mountain • Getting to Know You • The Glory of Love • Goodnight, My Someone • Medley from *The Phantom of the Opera* • Tomorrow • Yesterday.
00416709 Book/Audio...$12.99
00416693 Book Only..$7.99

FOURTH GRADE
10 all-time favorites: Chariots of Fire • Endless Love • Imagine • Mission: Impossible Theme • Moon River • On Broadway • Seasons of Love • Somewhere Out There • Till There Was You • A Whole New World.
00416710 Book/Audio...$12.99
00416694 Book Only..$7.99

FIFTH GRADE
10 great arrangements: Be Our Guest • Cabaret • Georgia on My Mind • In the Mood • Let It Be • Linus and Lucy • Puttin' On the Ritz • Under the Sea • The Way You Look Tonight • What a Wonderful World.
00416711 Book/Audio...$14.99
00416695 Book Only..$9.99

EXCLUSIVELY DISTRIBUTED BY

www.willispianomusic.com